PRAYER JOURNAL FOR BLACK WOMEN

52 WEEK DEVOTIONAL BETWEEN YOU AND GOD

Copyright © 2021 Stress Less Press.
All rights reserved. No part of this book may be reproduced or
transmitted in any form by any means, electronic or
mechanical, including photocopying, scanning and recording,
or by any information storage and retrieval system,
without permission in writing from the publisher,
except for the review for inclusion in a magazine, newspaper or broadcast.

OUR OTHER BOOKS FOR BLACK WOMEN

SELF CARE WORKBOOK FOR BLACK WOMEN
A 150+ page activity book covering mental, physical, spiritual and emotional self help practices. Complete with a 12-month planner and guided journal

EMOTIONAL SELF CARE FOR BLACK WOMEN
A self help activity book to address the thoughts, beliefs and triggers which affect your emotions and behavior

SPIRITUAL SELF CARE FOR BLACK WOMEN
A guided journal and 12-month planner with in-depth self reflection and spirituality activities

SELF CARE PLANNER & JOURNAL FOR BLACK WOMEN
A simple self care organizer and reflective journal

DREAM JOURNAL FOR BLACK WOMEN
Guided dream planner with prompts for you to interpret and reflect on your dreams

Stress Less Press are a Black-owned independent publisher. If you enjoy this book, please consider supporting us by leaving a review on Amazon!

LET'S GET INTO

Praying

INTRODUCTION
GIVE THANKS AND PRAY, SIS

How often do you sit in silence and reflect on what God is saying? How often do you give thanks and praises for the miracles that happen in your life? This journal has been designed for our Christian sisters who want to be more present in prayer, those who want to sit down, reflect and write.

Aside from the many studies that show journaling in general is a great stress reliever as you're able to reflect and work on yourself, specifically practicing prayer journaling allows you to share this self exploration with God. Over time you'll learn to know His voice and the direction, correction and inspiration he bestows upon you. Through this you'll soon find yourself having deeper and more meaningful conversations with Him. Keeping a prayer journal will also allow you to see how with gratitude, God works miracles in your life.

This journal will act as your personal record of your walk in faith, a place to write all your emotions, thoughts, doubts, questions, requests, the list is endless and it is up to you how deep you go. When you look back through your journal you'll see the personal growth you've experienced and the spiritual progress you've made.

You may already have an established praying routine and know your Bible verses line by line. If you don't and/or if you need inspiration for what to pray about, or want to consult the Bible on a specific topic to pray about, take inspiration from the 'Prayer Rolodex' that follows and start there.

Spend time in prayer, sit with Him and get your prayer game up. Start to receive answers to your prayers and develop a deeper understanding of the scripture, as well as a deeper relationship with God. In this prayer journal you'll find weekly wisdom throughout along with a focus on the following 4 key areas when praying: Gratitude, Lessons, Confession and Prayers for others.

Gratitude

Write about what you are grateful for that week, what has worked well for you and what or who has been a true blessing in your life. Use this space to reflect on what you give thanks for.

Lessons

What did the scripture teach you about yourself that week? What are you going to focus on in order to grow in faith? Write about it in this section.

Confession

Write about anything you need to confess to yourself and God in this section. If you feel you have dropped the ball with something, or someone, and need to get back on track, write it here and work on these things.

Prayers for others

Who do you want to pray for? Write their names and what you are praying for in this section. Praying for others is as important as praying for ourselves. God loves it when we are outward looking and put others first.

PRAYER *Rolodex*

SELF CARE

1 Corinthians 6:19-20
1 Corinthians 10:31
1 Corinthians 3:16
Psalm 46:5
Ephesians 5:18
Ephesians 5:29
Philippians 4:13
Proverbs 14:30
Romans 14:17-18
2 Timothy 1:7

LOVE

Romans 13:8
Matthew 22:37-39
Deuteronomy 7:9
1 Corinthians 13:4-8
1 Corinthians 16:14
John 3:16
Proverbs 10:12
Matthew 22:36-40
1 Corinthians 13:1-13
Ephesians 5:25

GRATITUDE

1 Thessalonians 5:16-18
Philippians 4:6-7
1 Corinthians 15:57
Romans 11:36
Colossians 3:17
Ephesians 5:29
Colossians 3:16
Luke 22:19
Revelation 5:13
Jonah 2:9

FAITH

Hebrews 11:11
Psalm 46:10
2 Corinthians 5:7
John 8:24
Luke 17:5
Hebrews 11:1
Ephesians 2:8-9
Proverbs 3:5-6
James 2:19
Mark 11:22-24

FORGIVENESS

1 John 1:9
Psalm 103:12
1 Corinthians 3:16
Ephesians 1:7
Daniel 9:9
Isaiah 43:25
Isaiah 1:18
Hebrews 10:17
Jeremiah 31:34
Luke 5:20

WISDOM

James 1:5
Psalm 90:12
Exodus 31:3
Proverbs 2:12
Ecclesiastes 7:12
Ephesians 5:29
Luke 21:15
James 3:13
Proverbs 24:14
1 Kings 4:29

COURAGE

1 Chronicles 28:20
Deuteronomy 31:6-8
Ephesians 6:10
Isaiah 54:4
Ephesians 5:18
John 14:27
Psalm 27:1
2 Timothy 1:7
Psalm 27:14
Mark 5:36

PROSPERITY

Deuteronomy 8:18
Philippians 4:19
Jeremiah 29:11
Malachi 3:10
Ephesians 5:18
1 Chronicles 4:10
Ecclesiastes 7:14
Genesis 15:1
Hosea 13:6
Jeremiah 17:10

PRAYERS FOR OTHERS

Matthew 6:7
1 John 5:14
Colossians 4:3-4
Psalm 17:6
Ephesians 6:18
Philippians 2:3-4
1 Timothy 2:1
James 5:16
John 14:13
Matthew 6:7

CHURCH & COMMUNITY

Matthew 6:7
1 John 1:7
1 Thessalonians 5:14
Colossians 3:13
James 5:16
Proverbs 17:17
Matthew 18:20
Romans 12:5
Hebrews 10:24-25
1 Peter 2:9-10

GRIEF / LOSS

John 16:22
Philippians 4:13
Revelation 21:4
Romans 8:18
Psalm 34:18
Matthew 11:28-30
Psalm 147:3
Matthew 5:1-3
Isaiah 53:4-6
Romans 12:2

OBEDIENCE

Exodus 19:5
Deuteronomy 11:1
Ephesians 6:1-3
2 Corinthians 10:5
John 15:9
Ephesians 6:1-3
Romans 1:5
John 15:14
Joshua 5:6
Luke 11:28

HUMILITY

Colossians 3:12
Ephesians 4:2
James 4:6
Luke 14:11
Micah 6:8
Proverbs 3:34
Psalm 25:9
Romans 12:16
Matthew 23:10-12
James 4:14-16

STRENGTH

Deuteronomy 31:6
Psalm 59:16
Jeremiah 32:17
Exodus 15:2
Psalm 119:28
1 Corinthians 16:13
Isaiah 40:29
Isaiah 41:10
Joshua 1:9
Psalm 27:1

KNOWLEDGE

Proverbs 2:6
Psalm 19:2
Proverbs 18:15
Isaiah 11:2
Proverbs 20:15
1 Corinthians 12:8
Ecclesiastes 1:18
Proverbs 11:9
2 Peter 3:18
1 Corinthians 13:2

RELATIONSHIPS

Proverbs 31:10-11
1 Peter 4:8
Colossians 3:19
Genesis 2:18
Ephesians 4:1-3
Proverbs 18:24
James 1:19-20
John 13:34
Ecclesiastes 7:8-9
1 Corinthians 6:18

TEMPTATION

James 1:13-18
Luke 22:40
John 8:6
Matthew 6:13
Luke 11:4
Luke 4:13
Matthew 4:7
Mark 8:11
Proverbs 7:25-26
1 Peter 4:12

CONFESSION

Proverbs 28:13
Psalm 32:5
Leviticus 5:5
Romans 10:10
Daniel 9:5
Romans 10:9
James 4:8
1 John 2:23
Acts 3:19
Romans 3:23-24

WEEKLY
wisdom

Rejoice always, pray continually, give thanks in all circumstances; for this is God's will for you in Christ Jesus.

1 THESSALONIANS
5: 16-18

reflections
JOURNAL

DATE: _____

GRATITUDE

_____
_____
_____
_____
_____
_____
_____
_____
_____
_____

LESSONS

CONFESSION

PRAYERS FOR OTHERS

_____
_____
_____
_____
_____
_____
_____
_____
_____
_____

WEEKLY *wisdom*

Do not be anxious about anything, but in every situation, by prayer and petition, with thanksgiving, present your requests to God. And the peace of God, which transcends all understanding, will guard your hearts and your minds in Christ Jesus.

PHILIPPIANS 4: 6-7

reflections
JOURNAL

DATE: _____

GRATITUDE

_____
_____
_____
_____
_____
_____
_____
_____
_____

LESSONS

CONFESSION

PRAYERS FOR OTHERS

_____
_____
_____
_____
_____
_____
_____
_____
_____
_____

WEEKLY
wisdom

This is the confidence we have in approaching God: that if we ask anything according to his will, he hears us.

1 JOHN
5:14-15

reflections
JOURNAL

DATE: _____

GRATITUDE

_____
_____
_____
_____
_____
_____
_____
_____
_____

LESSONS

CONFESSION

PRAYERS FOR OTHERS

_____
_____
_____
_____
_____
_____
_____
_____
_____
_____

WEEKLY
wisdom

Set your affection on things above, not on things on the earth.

COLOSSIANS 3:2

reflections
JOURNAL

DATE: _____

GRATITUDE

_____
_____
_____
_____
_____
_____
_____
_____
_____
_____

LESSONS

CONFESSION

PRAYERS FOR OTHERS

_____
_____
_____
_____
_____
_____
_____
_____
_____
_____
_____
_____

WEEKLY
wisdom

But to us there is but one God, the Father, of whom are all things, and we in him; and one Lord Jesus Christ, by whom are all things, and we by him.

1 CORINTHIANS 8:6

reflections
JOURNAL

DATE: _____

GRATITUDE

_____
_____
_____
_____
_____
_____
_____
_____
_____

LESSONS

CONFESSION

PRAYERS FOR OTHERS

_____
_____
_____
_____
_____
_____
_____
_____
_____
_____
_____

WEEKLY
wisdom

Rejoice in the Lord always: and again I say, Rejoice.

PHILIPPIANS 4:4

reflections
JOURNAL

DATE: _____

GRATITUDE

_____
_____
_____
_____
_____
_____
_____
_____
_____

LESSONS

CONFESSION

PRAYERS FOR OTHERS

_____
_____
_____
_____
_____
_____
_____
_____
_____
_____

WEEKLY
wisdom

Trust in the Lord with all thine heart; and lean not unto thine own understanding.

PROVERBS 3:5

reflections
JOURNAL

DATE: _____

GRATITUDE

_____
_____
_____
_____
_____
_____
_____
_____
_____

LESSONS

CONFESSION

PRAYERS FOR OTHERS

_____
_____
_____
_____
_____
_____
_____
_____
_____
_____
_____

WEEKLY
wisdom

Thou shalt have none other gods before me.

DEUTERONOMY
5:7

reflections
JOURNAL

DATE: _____

GRATITUDE

_____
_____
_____
_____
_____
_____
_____
_____
_____
_____

LESSONS

CONFESSION

PRAYERS FOR OTHERS

_____
_____
_____
_____
_____
_____
_____
_____
_____
_____

WEEKLY
wisdom

But to us there is but one God, the Father, of whom are all things, and we in him; and one Lord Jesus Christ, by whom are all things, and we by him.

1 CORINTHIANS 8:6

reflections
JOURNAL

DATE: _____

GRATITUDE

_____
_____
_____
_____
_____
_____
_____
_____
_____

LESSONS

CONFESSION

PRAYERS FOR OTHERS

_____
_____
_____
_____
_____
_____
_____
_____
_____
_____
_____

WEEKLY
wisdom

For whosoever shall call upon the name of the Lord shall be saved.

ROMANS 10:13

reflections
JOURNAL

DATE: _____

GRATITUDE

_____
_____
_____
_____
_____
_____
_____
_____
_____

LESSONS

CONFESSION

PRAYERS FOR OTHERS

_____
_____
_____
_____
_____
_____
_____
_____
_____
_____

WEEKLY *wisdom*

Devote yourselves to prayer, being watchful and thankful.

COLOSSIANS 4:2

reflections
JOURNAL

DATE: _____

GRATITUDE

_____
_____
_____
_____
_____
_____
_____
_____
_____
_____

LESSONS

CONFESSION

PRAYERS FOR OTHERS

_____
_____
_____
_____
_____
_____
_____
_____
_____
_____
_____

WEEKLY
wisdom

Therefore I tell you, whatever you ask for in prayer, believe that you have received it, and it will be yours.

MARK 11:24

reflections
JOURNAL

DATE: _____

GRATITUDE

_____
_____
_____
_____
_____
_____
_____
_____
_____

LESSONS

CONFESSION

PRAYERS FOR OTHERS

_____
_____
_____
_____
_____
_____
_____
_____
_____
_____

WEEKLY
wisdom

Call to me and I will answer you and tell you great and unsearchable things you do not know.

JEREMIAH 33:3

reflections
JOURNAL

DATE: _____

GRATITUDE

_____
_____
_____
_____
_____
_____
_____
_____
_____

LESSONS

CONFESSION

PRAYERS FOR OTHERS

_____
_____
_____
_____
_____
_____
_____
_____
_____
_____

WEEKLY *wisdom*

But when you pray, go into your room, close the door and pray to your Father, who is unseen. Then your Father, who sees what is done in secret, will reward you.

MATTHEW 6:6

reflections
JOURNAL

DATE: _____

GRATITUDE

_____
_____
_____
_____
_____
_____
_____
_____
_____

LESSONS

CONFESSION

PRAYERS FOR OTHERS

_____
_____
_____
_____
_____
_____
_____
_____
_____
_____

WEEKLY
wisdom

But to you who are listening I say: Love your enemies, do good to those who hate you, bless those who curse you, pray for those who mistreat you.

LUKE 6:27-28

reflections
JOURNAL

DATE: _____

GRATITUDE

_____
_____
_____
_____
_____
_____
_____
_____
_____
_____

LESSONS

CONFESSION

PRAYERS FOR OTHERS

_____
_____
_____
_____
_____
_____
_____
_____
_____
_____

WEEKLY
wisdom

Look to the LORD and his strength; seek his face always.

1 CHRONICLES 16:11

reflections
JOURNAL

DATE: _____

GRATITUDE

_____
_____
_____
_____
_____
_____
_____
_____
_____

LESSONS

CONFESSION

PRAYERS FOR OTHERS

_____
_____
_____
_____
_____
_____
_____
_____
_____
_____
_____

WEEKLY
wisdom

If my people, who are called by my name, will humble themselves and pray and seek my face and turn from their wicked ways, then I will hear from heaven, and I will forgive their sin and will heal their land.

2 CHRONICLES 7:14

reflections
JOURNAL

DATE: _____

GRATITUDE

_____
_____
_____
_____
_____
_____
_____
_____
_____
_____

LESSONS

CONFESSION

PRAYERS FOR OTHERS

_____
_____
_____
_____
_____
_____
_____
_____
_____
_____

WEEKLY
wisdom

Therefore I tell you, whatever you ask for in prayer, believe that you have received it, and it will be

MARK 11:24

reflections
JOURNAL

DATE: _____

GRATITUDE

_____
_____
_____
_____
_____
_____
_____
_____
_____
_____

LESSONS

CONFESSION

PRAYERS FOR OTHERS

_____
_____
_____
_____
_____
_____
_____
_____
_____
_____

WEEKLY
wisdom

> But I tell you, love your enemies and pray for those who persecute you,

MATTHEW 5:44

reflections
JOURNAL

DATE: _____

GRATITUDE

_____
_____
_____
_____
_____
_____
_____
_____
_____

LESSONS

CONFESSION

PRAYERS FOR OTHERS

_____
_____
_____
_____
_____
_____
_____
_____
_____
_____

WEEKLY *wisdom*

> Watch and pray so that you will not fall into temptation. The spirit is willing, but the flesh is weak.

MATTHEW 26:41

reflections
JOURNAL

DATE: _____

GRATITUDE

_____
_____
_____
_____
_____
_____
_____
_____
_____

LESSONS

CONFESSION

PRAYERS FOR OTHERS

_____
_____
_____
_____
_____
_____
_____
_____
_____
_____
_____

WEEKLY
wisdom

May my prayer be set before you like incense; may the lifting up of my hands be like the evening sacrifice.

PSALM 141:2

reflections
JOURNAL

DATE: _____

GRATITUDE

_____
_____
_____
_____
_____
_____
_____
_____
_____
_____

LESSONS

CONFESSION

PRAYERS FOR OTHERS

_____
_____
_____
_____
_____
_____
_____
_____
_____
_____

WEEKLY
wisdom

This is the day which the Lord hath made; we will rejoice and be glad in it.

PSALM 118:24

reflections
JOURNAL

DATE: _____

GRATITUDE

_____
_____
_____
_____
_____
_____
_____
_____
_____
_____

LESSONS

CONFESSION

PRAYERS FOR OTHERS

_____
_____
_____
_____
_____
_____
_____
_____
_____
_____
_____

WEEKLY
wisdom

Thy word is a lamp unto my feet, and a light unto my path.

PSALM 119:105

reflections
JOURNAL

DATE: _____

GRATITUDE

_____
_____
_____
_____
_____
_____
_____
_____
_____
_____

LESSONS

CONFESSION

PRAYERS FOR OTHERS

_____
_____
_____
_____
_____
_____
_____
_____
_____
_____
_____

WEEKLY
wisdom

The Lord bless thee, and keep thee: The Lord make his face shine upon thee, and be gracious unto thee: The Lord lift up his countenance upon thee, and give thee peace.

NUMBERS 6:24-26

reflections
JOURNAL

DATE: _____

GRATITUDE

_____
_____
_____
_____
_____
_____
_____
_____
_____
_____

LESSONS

CONFESSION

PRAYERS FOR OTHERS

_____
_____
_____
_____
_____
_____
_____
_____
_____
_____

WEEKLY *wisdom*

Commit thy works unto the Lord, and thy thoughts shall be established.

PROVERBS 16:3

reflections
JOURNAL

DATE: _____

GRATITUDE

_____
_____
_____
_____
_____
_____
_____
_____
_____

LESSONS

CONFESSION

PRAYERS FOR OTHERS

_____
_____
_____
_____
_____
_____
_____
_____
_____
_____
_____

WEEKLY *wisdom*

Fear thou not; for I am with thee: be not dismayed; for I am thy God: I will strengthen thee; yea, I will help thee; yea, I will uphold thee with the right hand of my righteousness.

ISAIAH 41:10

reflections
JOURNAL

DATE: _____

GRATITUDE

_____
_____
_____
_____
_____
_____
_____
_____
_____

LESSONS

CONFESSION

PRAYERS FOR OTHERS

_____
_____
_____
_____
_____
_____
_____
_____
_____
_____

WEEKLY *wisdom*

And ye shall serve the Lord your God, and he shall bless thy bread, and thy water; and I will take sickness away from the midst of thee.

EXODUS 23:25

reflections
JOURNAL

DATE: _____

GRATITUDE

_____
_____
_____
_____
_____
_____
_____
_____
_____
_____

LESSONS

CONFESSION

PRAYERS FOR OTHERS

_____
_____
_____
_____
_____
_____
_____
_____
_____
_____

WEEKLY
wisdom

For we walk by faith,
not by sight.

2 CORINTHIANS
5:7

reflections
JOURNAL

DATE: _____

GRATITUDE

_____
_____
_____
_____
_____
_____
_____
_____
_____

LESSONS

CONFESSION

PRAYERS FOR OTHERS

_____
_____
_____
_____
_____
_____
_____
_____
_____

WEEKLY *wisdom*

And whatsoever ye do, do it heartily, as to the Lord, and not unto men; Knowing that of the Lord ye shall receive the reward of the inheritance: for ye serve the Lord Christ.

COLOSSIANS 3:23-24

reflections
JOURNAL

DATE: _____

GRATITUDE

_____
_____
_____
_____
_____
_____
_____
_____
_____

LESSONS

CONFESSION

PRAYERS FOR OTHERS

_____
_____
_____
_____
_____
_____
_____
_____
_____
_____

WEEKLY
wisdom

Grant thee according to thine own heart, and fulfil all thy counsel.

PSALM 20:4

reflections
JOURNAL

DATE: _____

GRATITUDE

_____
_____
_____
_____
_____
_____
_____
_____
_____
_____

LESSONS

CONFESSION

PRAYERS FOR OTHERS

_____
_____
_____
_____
_____
_____
_____
_____
_____
_____
_____

WEEKLY *wisdom*

Jesus Christ is the same yesterday and today and forever.

HEBREWS 13:8

reflections
JOURNAL

DATE: _____

GRATITUDE

_____
_____
_____
_____
_____
_____
_____
_____
_____
_____

LESSONS

CONFESSION

PRAYERS FOR OTHERS

_____
_____
_____
_____
_____
_____
_____
_____
_____
_____
_____

WEEKLY *wisdom*

Seek the LORD and his strength; seek his presence continually!

1 CHRONICLES 16:11

reflections
JOURNAL

DATE: _____

GRATITUDE

_____
_____
_____
_____
_____
_____
_____
_____
_____

LESSONS

CONFESSION

PRAYERS FOR OTHERS

_____
_____
_____
_____
_____
_____
_____
_____
_____
_____

WEEKLY
wisdom

When I am afraid, I put my trust in you.

PSALM 56:3

reflections
JOURNAL

DATE: _____

GRATITUDE

_____
_____
_____
_____
_____
_____
_____
_____
_____
_____

LESSONS

CONFESSION

PRAYERS FOR OTHERS

_____
_____
_____
_____
_____
_____
_____
_____
_____
_____

WEEKLY *wisdom*

Trust in the LORD, and do good; dwell in the land and befriend faithfulness

PSALM 37:3

reflections
JOURNAL

DATE: _____

GRATITUDE

LESSONS

CONFESSION

PRAYERS FOR OTHERS

WEEKLY
wisdom

Look to the LORD and his strength; seek his face always.

1 CHRONICLES 16:11

reflections
JOURNAL

DATE: _____

GRATITUDE

_____
_____
_____
_____
_____
_____
_____
_____
_____

LESSONS

CONFESSION

PRAYERS FOR OTHERS

_____
_____
_____
_____
_____
_____
_____
_____
_____
_____

WEEKLY
wisdom

Yet for us there is but one God, the Father, from whom all things came and for whom we live; and there is but one Lord, Jesus Christ, through whom all things came and through whom we live.

1 CORINTHIANS 8:6

reflections
JOURNAL

DATE: _____

GRATITUDE
_____
_____
_____
_____
_____
_____
_____
_____
_____

LESSONS

CONFESSION

PRAYERS FOR OTHERS
_____
_____
_____
_____
_____
_____
_____
_____
_____
_____

WEEKLY
wisdom

For the Spirit God gave us does not make us timid, but gives us power, love and self-discipline.

2 TIMOTHY 1:7

reflections
JOURNAL

DATE: _____

GRATITUDE

_____
_____
_____
_____
_____
_____
_____
_____
_____

LESSONS

CONFESSION

PRAYERS FOR OTHERS

_____
_____
_____
_____
_____
_____
_____
_____
_____
_____
_____

WEEKLY
wisdom

Be kind and compassionate to one another, forgiving each other, just as in Christ God forgave you.

EPHESIANS 4:32

reflections
JOURNAL

DATE: _____

GRATITUDE

_____
_____
_____
_____
_____
_____
_____
_____
_____
_____

LESSONS

CONFESSION

PRAYERS FOR OTHERS

_____
_____
_____
_____
_____
_____
_____
_____
_____
_____

WEEKLY
wisdom

For I know the plans I have for you," declares the LORD, "plans to prosper you and not to harm you, plans to give you hope and a future.

JEREMIAH 29:11

reflections
JOURNAL

DATE: _____

GRATITUDE

_____
_____
_____
_____
_____
_____
_____
_____
_____

LESSONS

CONFESSION

PRAYERS FOR OTHERS

_____
_____
_____
_____
_____
_____
_____
_____
_____
_____
_____

WEEKLY
wisdom

For God so loved the world that he gave his one and only Son, that whoever believes in him shall not perish but have eternal life.

JOHN 3:16

reflections
JOURNAL

DATE: _____

GRATITUDE

_____
_____
_____
_____
_____
_____
_____
_____
_____
_____

LESSONS

CONFESSION

PRAYERS FOR OTHERS

_____
_____
_____
_____
_____
_____
_____
_____
_____
_____
_____

WEEKLY
wisdom

You are the light of the world. A town built on a hill cannot be hidden.

MATTHEW 5:14

reflections
JOURNAL

DATE: _____

GRATITUDE

_____
_____
_____
_____
_____
_____
_____
_____
_____

LESSONS

CONFESSION

PRAYERS FOR OTHERS

_____
_____
_____
_____
_____
_____
_____
_____
_____
_____

WEEKLY *wisdom*

The LORD makes firm the steps of the one who delights in him; though he may stumble, he will not fall, for the LORD upholds him with his hand.

PSALM 37:23-24

reflections
JOURNAL

DATE: _____

GRATITUDE

_____
_____
_____
_____
_____
_____
_____
_____
_____
_____

LESSONS

CONFESSION

PRAYERS FOR OTHERS

_____
_____
_____
_____
_____
_____
_____
_____
_____
_____

WEEKLY
wisdom

And the peace of God, which transcends all understanding, will guard your hearts and your minds in Christ Jesus.

PHILIPPIANS 4:7

reflections
JOURNAL

DATE: _____

GRATITUDE

_____
_____
_____
_____
_____
_____
_____
_____
_____
_____

LESSONS

CONFESSION

PRAYERS FOR OTHERS

_____
_____
_____
_____
_____
_____
_____
_____
_____
_____

WEEKLY
wisdom

Be strong and courageous. Do not be afraid or terrified because of them, for the LORD your God goes with you; he will never leave you nor forsake you

DEUTERONOMY 31:6

reflections
JOURNAL

DATE: _____

GRATITUDE

_____
_____
_____
_____
_____
_____
_____
_____
_____
_____

LESSONS

CONFESSION

PRAYERS FOR OTHERS

_____
_____
_____
_____
_____
_____
_____
_____
_____
_____

WEEKLY
wisdom

You, dear children, are from God and have overcome them, because the one who is in you is greater than the one who is in the world.

1 JOHN 4:4

reflections
JOURNAL

DATE: _____

GRATITUDE

_____
_____
_____
_____
_____
_____
_____
_____
_____
_____

LESSONS

CONFESSION

PRAYERS FOR OTHERS

_____
_____
_____
_____
_____
_____
_____
_____
_____
_____
_____
_____

WEEKLY
wisdom

I keep my eyes always on the LORD. With him at my right hand, I shall not be shaken.

PSALM 16:8

reflections
JOURNAL

DATE: _____

GRATITUDE

_____
_____
_____
_____
_____
_____
_____
_____
_____
_____

LESSONS

CONFESSION

PRAYERS FOR OTHERS

_____
_____
_____
_____
_____
_____
_____
_____
_____
_____
_____

WEEKLY
wisdom

For no word from God
will ever fail.

LUKE
1:37

reflections
JOURNAL

DATE: _____

GRATITUDE
_____
_____
_____
_____
_____
_____
_____
_____
_____

LESSONS

CONFESSION

PRAYERS FOR OTHERS
_____
_____
_____
_____
_____
_____
_____
_____
_____
_____

WEEKLY
wisdom

Rejoicing in hope, patient in tribulation, continuing steadfastly in prayer.

ROMANS 12:12

reflections
JOURNAL

DATE: _____

GRATITUDE

_____
_____
_____
_____
_____
_____
_____
_____
_____
_____

LESSONS

CONFESSION

PRAYERS FOR OTHERS

_____
_____
_____
_____
_____
_____
_____
_____
_____
_____

WEEKLY
wisdom

The name of the Lord is a strong tower; The righteous run to it and are safe.

PROVERBS
18:10

reflections
JOURNAL

DATE: _____

GRATITUDE
_____
_____
_____
_____
_____
_____
_____
_____
_____
_____

LESSONS

CONFESSION

PRAYERS FOR OTHERS
_____
_____
_____
_____
_____
_____
_____
_____
_____
_____

WEEKLY
wisdom

Let the words of my mouth and
the meditation of my heart
Be acceptable in Your sight.

PSALM
19:14

reflections
JOURNAL

DATE: _____

GRATITUDE

_____
_____
_____
_____
_____
_____
_____
_____
_____
_____

LESSONS

CONFESSION

PRAYERS FOR OTHERS

_____
_____
_____
_____
_____
_____
_____
_____
_____
_____
_____

WEEKLY
wisdom

Now faith is confidence in what we hope for and assurance about what we do not see.

HEBREWS 11:1

reflections
JOURNAL

DATE: _____

GRATITUDE

_____
_____
_____
_____
_____
_____
_____
_____
_____
_____

LESSONS

CONFESSION

PRAYERS FOR OTHERS

_____
_____
_____
_____
_____
_____
_____
_____
_____
_____

WEEKLY
wisdom

...but those who hope in the LORD will renew their strength. They will soar on wings like eagles; they will run and not grow weary, they will walk and not be faint.

ISAIAH 40:31

reflections
JOURNAL

DATE: _____

GRATITUDE

_____
_____
_____
_____
_____
_____
_____
_____
_____
_____

LESSONS

CONFESSION

PRAYERS FOR OTHERS

_____
_____
_____
_____
_____
_____
_____
_____
_____
_____

WEEKLY *wisdom*

Praise be to the LORD for He has heard my cry for mercy. The LORD is my strength and my shield; my heart trusts in him, and he helps me. My heart leaps for joy, and with my song I praise him.

PSALM 28:6-7

reflections
JOURNAL

DATE: _____

GRATITUDE

_____
_____
_____
_____
_____
_____
_____
_____
_____
_____

LESSONS

CONFESSION

PRAYERS FOR OTHERS

_____
_____
_____
_____
_____
_____
_____
_____
_____
_____

JOURNAL
pages

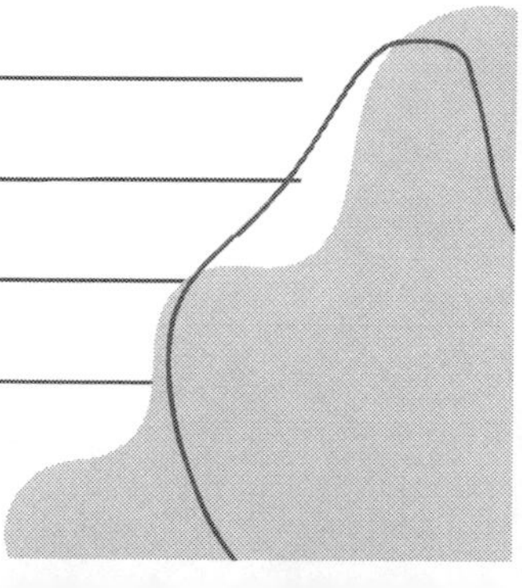

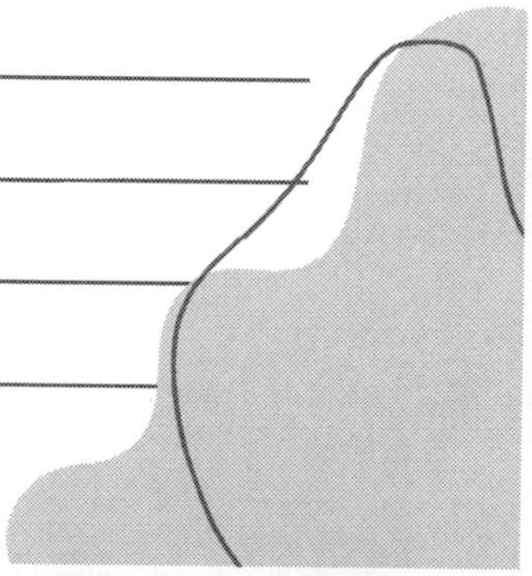

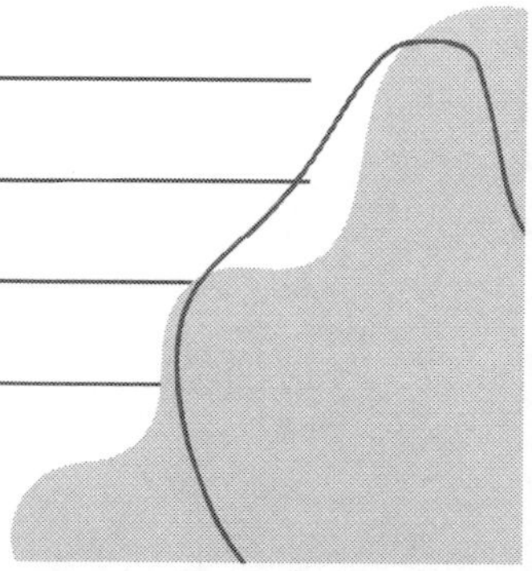

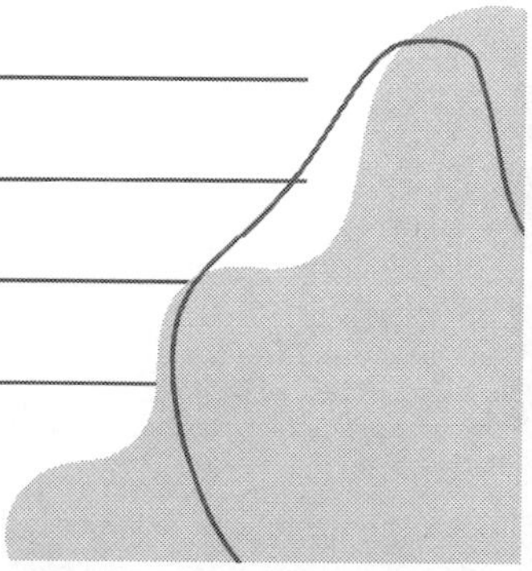

Made in the USA
Columbia, SC
06 January 2025